Joan Rivers and Bergdorf Goodman

A Play in Two Acts by

Louis E.V. Nevaer

A dark comedy about AIDS and friendship

Based on a true act of kindness in a time of pestilence.

JOAN RIVERS AND BERGDORG GOODMAN
Copyright 2014 by Louis E.V. Nevaer

Publication date: December 2014

ISBN 978-1-939879-18-9

Contact publisher for additional copies and performance rights information:

> Hispanic Economics, Inc.
> P.O. Box 140681
> Coral Gables, FL 33114-0681
> *info@hispaniceconomics.com*

Cover and interior design by John Clifton
johnclifton.net

DEDICATION

Joan Alexandra Molinsky

SYNOPSIS

Mark Hopkinson, a jewelry salesman at Bergdorf Goodman, lavishes attention on his favorite client, Joan Rivers. That is, until he becomes sick with a series of diseases that, in 1988, are still dismissed as the "gay plague," although the syndrome has a name: AIDS. When he becomes too ill to work, Joan Rivers confronts the staff at Bergdorf Goodman, demanding they give her his telephone number. It is only after she makes a scene on the sales floor that they relent just to get her out of the store.

Mark Hopkinson, who quickly comes down with full-blown AIDS, is treated like a pariah by coworkers and family alike. Joan Rivers, although despondent over her husband's suicide, her daughter's subsequent refusal to speak to her, and setbacks in her career, is determined to help Mark Hopkinson. Their unlikely friendship centers on the existential anguish both feel at this point in their lives. Their relationship is one of extraordinary kindness at a time when the world is confronting a terrifying and deadly pestilence.

CAST OF CHARACTERS

JOAN RIVERS, a comedian in her 50s

MARK HOPKINSON, a salesperson in his 30s

DALE NORTON, a salesperson in his 40s

HEATHER BURKE, a salesperson in her 20s

CONSUELO RODRÍGUEZ, a housekeeper in her 40s

SETTING

The action takes place in Bergdorf Goodman Department

Store, New York City

and the apartment of Mark Hopkinson

in Greenwich Village, New York.

The time is 1988.

SYNOPSIS OF SCENES

Act I

Scene 1

Bergdorf Goodman department store, New York.

1988. MARK HOPKINSON, *a salesman in the Bergdorf Goodman jewelry department, is setting aside pieces of jewelry for a client. He is speaking to a colleague,* DALE NORTON, *in a hurried manner.*

HOPKINSON. Now, remember, these pieces are for Joan—the ones she definitely wants. And these are the ones I think would look fabulous on her. Got that?

NORTON. *(Annoyed.)* Yes, I get it. It's not that difficult.

HOPKINSON. I just get nervous—and I do appreciate your coming over here, Dale. I know this isn't your department.

NORTON. It's not a problem, Mark. But you won't be long, will you?

HOPKINSON. I'm just dropping off some insurance forms at the doctor's office; I plan to be back in ten minutes. *(Pause.)* I don't remember if she said she'd drop by at four, or was it three? *(Looking up at* NORTON.*)* In any case, my doctor's office is around the corner and I won't be long.

NORTON. *(With concern.)* Are you all right, Mark? You seem to be coming to the shoe department pretty often for one of us to fill in for you.

HOPKINSON. Oh, I'm fine. It's just that I can't seem to shake off this cough. That's all.

NORTON. You've had that respiratory thing for some time now, haven't you?

HOPKINSON. I know. It's odd.

(The men look at each other for a moment.)

NORTON. Yes, it is odd. *(Pause.)* I just hope you get over it soon.

HOPKINSON. Me, too! But remember, you have to treat Joan like the star that she is! And I'll be back before you know it.

(HOPKINSON *exits, with a small folder of papers, while* NORTON *looks at him.)*

NORTON. I hope he's all right. *(He fusses with the trays of jewelry, and then he picks up the house telephone and dials.)* Hello, Heather? It's Dale. You'll never guess what, princess? Well, Mark is off to see his doctor or something...Yes, I know, again...But listen to this, princess. He has some jewelry set aside for Joan! *(Pause.)* Can you believe it? *(Pause.)* It has to be her! Mark said to treat her like the star that she is. *(Pause.)* Isn't this exciting! I'll call you the moment she shows up so you can come down. I mean, it isn't every day that Joan Collins is in the store! *(Pause.)* Well, of course it has to be her! What other star in the world is named Joan? Crawford's dead! *(Looking at the price tags.)* And besides, these pieces are fabulous. One's $19,000, another is $27,500, and the third is $47,000! These are pieces worthy of her! *(Pause.)* Oh, did you see last week's episode? I tell you, princess, *Dynasty* becomes better and better each season. Joan Collins is the *perfect* Alexis Carrington, absolutely fabulous! *(*NORTON *continues to speak into the receiver in a conspiratorial manner and is oblivious to* JOAN RIVERS *entering the department.)* You must come up with an excuse to come down when I call you, princess! I know you think Linda Evans is a better actress, but you simply must listen to this gay man's verdict: Joan Collins rules!

(JOAN RIVERS *approaches and clears her throat to get* NORTON'*s attention.)*

RIVERS. Excuse me, where's Mr. Hopkinson?

NORTON. *(In a dismissive manner, not recognizing her.)* He's not here, ma'am. He should be back shortly. *(He turns his back to her, continuing to whisper into the telephone receiver.)*

RIVERS. Excuse me, but I'm here—and I'm a customer.

NORTON. *(Turns around, annoyed.)* Ma'am, I said that Mr. Hopkinson will return shortly. You can wait for him if you like.

RIVERS. No. I don't have time. And I'm the customer, so that means that I'm always right because the customer is always right.

NORTON. *(Annoyed, putting his hand over the telephone receiver.)* I'm afraid this isn't my regular department, but if you can wait, Mr. Hopkinson will return shortly.

RIVERS. No, no, no, no, no! I'm the customer! The customer is always right! Mark told me he's set aside some pieces for me.

NORTON. *(Speaking into the telephone receiver.)* Heather, let me call you back in a moment. *(To RIVERS.)* Excuse me, but did you say that Mark set aside some pieces for you?

RIVERS. Of course, that's what I just said. I told him I'd be here at three and he said that if had to rush out to the doctor's office, he'd leave the three pieces for me.

NORTON. *(Confused.)* And your name?

RIVERS. My name? What's the matter with you? You don't know who I am?

NORTON. *(Slowly.)* Joan?

RIVERS. *(Slowly.)* Yes, it's me: Joan Rivers. But I prefer to be called by my married name, Mrs. Rosenberg.

NORTON. *(Regaining his professional composure.)* Yes, of course, Mrs. Rosenberg. I'm sorry—I just didn't recognize you!

RIVERS. *(Slowly.)* Yes, I'm trying not to be recognized. I'm still not doing well since my husband's suicide.

NORTON. *(Clearing his throat.)* Of course, it's understandable, Mrs. Rosenberg. Your husband was a wonderful man. It was all very tragic. I couldn't help but read all about it in the papers and magazines.

RIVERS. You have no idea what a wonderful man Edgar Rosenberg was, but I'm still furious that he took his own life.

NORTON. *(Reaching for the case with the jewels set aside for her.)* Yes, of course, Mrs. Rosenberg. *(Pause.)* Now, here are the three stunning pieces that Mr. Hopkinson set aside for your consideration. *(Reaching for a smaller tray.)* And this tray has two other pieces that, in Mr. Hopkinson's opinion, would look absolutely fabulous on you.

RIVERS. *(Reaching for one of the pieces, as NORTON helps her.)* Thank, you...Mr.?

NORTON. *(Slowly.)* Norton. Dale Norton, Mrs. Rosenberg.

RIVERS. *(Smiling.)* Yes, Mr. Norton. *(Pauses as she looks in the mirror to admire the jewelry on her.)* I sense disappointment on your part.

NORTON. *(Surprised.)* Why? What would lead you to say such a thing? I'm delighted to attend to you.

RIVERS. *(Smiling.)* No, you are not, Mr. Norton. Let me tell you something. I've been around long enough to sense a man's disappointment in me—even if that man is not interested in women. *(Raising her hand.)* Before you protest, I don't care. *(Admiring the piece in the mirror.)* For decades I've been a fag hag...Oh, God, how I that that phrase! Fag hag! I hate it! But I have to be honest and I have to admit, that's what I am. *(Pause.)* Can we talk Mr. Norton? I know disappointment when I see it, and not just because I am a fag hag. I'm very familiar with any man's disappointment in me. *(Pause.)* I'm not the Joan you were expecting, am I?

*(*HOPKINSON *enters in a rushed manner. Putting his gloves on the counter, he addresses* RIVERS *directly.)*

HOPKINSON. *(Animated.)* Oh, Joan, I'm so sorry I'm late! I had to drop off paperwork at the doctor's office.

RIVERS. *(Reaching to kiss him on the cheek.)* Mark, not to worry! I'm happy to see you.

HOPKINSON. *(To* NORTON.*)* Thank you, Dale, for holding down the fort.

NORTON. Not a problem, Mark. I'll leave you to your customer. *(To* RIVERS.*)* It's been a pleasure, Mrs. Rosenberg.

RIVERS. I wish it could have been more of a pleasure for me!

*(*NORTON *pats* HOPKINSON *on the back as he exits.)*

HOPKINSON. *(Looking at* NORTON *first, then* RIVERS.*)* What was that all about?

RIVERS. The story of my life: Failing to meet a man's expectation of me!

HOPKINSON. Oh, you're being ridiculous, Joan! You have never failed to meet my expectations! *(They look at each other.)* Now, aren't these pieces fabulous?

RIVERS. Gorgeous, Mark! They are gorgeous!

HOPKINSON. Isn't that what I told you?

RIVERS. *(Turning to look in the direction of* NORTON's *exit.)* You're terribly kind to me, Mark. But somehow, I think I disappointed your colleague, Mr. Norton.

HOPKINSON. *(Raising his eyebrows in a dismissive way.)* Don't worry about it, Joan. Dale's always hoping Joan Crawford walks in!

RIVERS. *(Laughing.)* And instead, he got *this* mummy!

Scene 2

Mark Hopkinson's apartment. Greenwich Village, New York.

A small studio apartment in Greenwich Village. There is a large framed poster of Andy Warhol's advertising for Halston. There are framed photographs of Bette Davis, Greta Garbo, Joan Crawford, and Madonna on the wall over an Art Deco exotic burl and onyx sideboard buffet. Two Art Deco leather club chairs and a stylish Art Deco occasional table are in the center of the room. The decor is understated and tasteful. CONSUELO RODRÍGUEZ, *who comes in twice a week, is tidying things up.* MARK HOPKINSON *enters.*

RODRÍGUEZ. Mr. Mark, you're home early.

HOPKINSON. *(Clearing his throat.)* Yes, I wasn't feeling well, and I just decided to come home early and rest.

RODRÍGUEZ. That cold of yours, it won't go away.

HOPKINSON. I know. I've been to several doctors, and they don't know why it won't go away.

RODRÍGUEZ. Well, you should be careful. I remember when my grandmother came down with a terrible cold three years ago. It developed into pneumonia. It almost killed her.

HOPKINSON. Consuelo, I think if I came down with pneumonia, I could tackle it. I mean, with all due respect, your grandmother is at least half a century older than me!

RODRÍGUEZ. I know, Mr. Mark. I'm just saying with things the way they are in today's world...

HOPKINSON. What do you mean?

RODRÍGUEZ. Reading the news, I can't believe some of the things happening.

HOPKINSON. Such as what?

RODRÍGUEZ. I mean, I still can't believe Rock Hudson is dead. It seems like yesterday. And from that disease that's going around that no one knows anything about. Some call it an epidemic, others call it a pandemic. I've heard it's like a plague. The couple whose house I clean every Friday told me that they had stopped eating out at restaurants. She said a doctor told her it could spread on dinnerware if the utensils are not properly washed. I thought she was exaggerating, but then Rock Hudson died. *(Pause.)* I remember as a young girl how I had a crush on him when *Pillow Talk* came out. He and Doris Day were so perfect together. And then he comes down with all those strange diseases. *(Pause.)* They say it came from chimpanzees in Africa. A chimpanzee bit someone and instead of giving him rabies, he gave him that killer virus. *(She reaches for chocolates on a plate on the occasional table and eats a couple of bonbons.)* It's all very frightening. At my medical assistant school the instructors tell us that guidelines for nursing staff have been revised. Everyone is starting to wear gloves when touching any patient. *(Pause.)* We can cure rabies, but who can tell about killer viruses from the African tropics?

HOPKINSON. Consuelo, it has a name. It's an immune deficiency disorder and it's transmitted through intimate sexual contact and bodily fluids. It's called Acquired Immune Deficiency Syndrome. AIDS. You should know that. Isn't that taught at the medical assistant school you're attending? *(In a defensive manner.)* And what does that have to do with anything?

RODRÍGUEZ. *(Humbled, offering the plate of chocolates to* HOPKINSON, *who declines.)* Nothing, Mr. Mark. It's just that, nowadays, all kinds of diseases travel around the world on airplanes. Infected passengers spread disease everywhere they land. Today it's a virus from Africa. A few years ago it was a flu infection from China. Who knows what's next? *(Pause.)* I'm just concerned your cough hasn't gone away. *(Pause.)* Are you constipated?

HOPKINSON. No, I'm not constipated.

RODRÍGUEZ. *(Animated.)* Because if you are, I can

prepare a solution, like last time. Enemas are very healthy. I was reading about their holistic benefits in *Selecciones del Reader's Digest.* I also was told that Princess Diana loves them. They call them "colonic irrigation" in England.

HOPKINSON. That's all very interesting, Consuelo, but I don't think that an enema would solve my medical problems.

RODRÍGUEZ. Okay, Mr. Mark. But like my *mamacita* always said, "Anyone who does not have a proper bowl movement—"

HOPKINSON. "—is full of shit." I know. *(Apologetically.)* I'm sorry, I don't mean to be testy, Consuelo. It's just that I'm frustrated by this...this, *whatever* this is. *(Pause.)* I just can't wait for it to go away.

RODRÍGUEZ. *(Turning to leave.)* I rolled a joint for you, like you asked. It's in your study.

HOPKINSON. Oh, thank you. On days like today, I need some pot.

RODRÍGUEZ. Don't smoke too much; it isn't good for your cough! *(Pause.)* Oh, I also left the mail on your desk, Mr. Mark. And I'll stop by the dry cleaners when I come back on Thursday. Is there anything else?

HOPKINSON. *(Slightly distracted.)* No, that's all. *(Pause.)* I just need to rest, Consuelo. Then I'll be fine.

RODRÍGUEZ. I made soup for you, Mr. Mark. It's on the stove. Fresh chicken soup. I made the stock myself this afternoon.

HOPKINSON. That was kind of you. *(Walking over to put on some music.)* Where's the George Michael CD?

RODRÍGUEZ. *(Stopping, pointing to the sideboard buffet.)* Right where you left it, on that credenza.

HOPKINSON. *(Singing.)* 'Cause I've got to have faith. *(Turning to her.)* You have a good evening, Consuelo.

RODRÍGUEZ. *(As she exits.)* Good night, Mr. Mark.

HOPKINSON. *(Singing.)* Faith, faith. I've got to have faith.

Scene 3

Bergdorf Goodman department store, New York.

DALE NORTON *is assisting* HEATHER BURKE *in the jewelry department. The two are arranging various pieces of jewelry on several trays.*

> BURKE. Must be nice to have management allow such liberal working hours.
>
> NORTON. *(Annoyed.)* Wish I could just saunter on in whenever I wanted—knowing others would pick up the slack.
>
> BURKE. Speaking of being a slacker, you never called me back when Joan Collins was here.
>
> NORTON. *(Stopping and looking straight at her.)* It wasn't Joan Collins, princess. It was Joan Rivers.
>
> BURKE. *(Disappointed.)* That has-been?
>
> NORTON. Exactly. Fox canceled her show last year, *The Late Show Starring Joan Rivers*, or whatever it was called. And her husband killed himself soon after that. I heard her daughter won't speak to her anymore. And on top of everything...*(in a conspiratorial whisper)* she looks terrible.
>
> BURKE. Well, if that's the case, then I'm glad I didn't waste my time coming down. *(Pause.)* But still, I was so excited about seeing Joan Collins!
>
> NORTON. Do you know something?
>
> BURKE. What?
>
> NORTON. Isn't fate odd?
>
> BURKE. What do you mean?
>
> NORTON. Well, Joan Collins and Joan Rivers were born the same year. And Joan Collins is a goddess—and Joan Rivers...*isn't*!
>
> BURKE. *(Laughing.)* Is that right? They're the same age!
>
> (HOPKINSON *enters and walks toward* NORTON *and* BURKE.)

HOPKINSON. *(In a cheerful manner.)* Good afternoon, Dale! Hello, gorgeous Heather!

NORTON. *(Looking up.)* Oh, you're back, Mark. I'm glad.

HOPKINSON. Thank you so much for helping me with the display.

BURKE. It's our pleasure.

NORTON. *(Putting down a tray of jewelry.)* Well, Mark, now that you're here, I'll go back to the shoe department. You never know when a princess will walk in wanting to try on a glass slipper!

(NORTON exits.)

BURKE. He's very nice.

HOPKINSON. *(Selecting pieces and putting them on a tray.)* And I do appreciate you and Dale covering for me. I owe you. As soon as I'm back to my healthy self, I'll pay you both back with my vacation time.

BURKE. You don't have to, Mark. *(Pause.)* What are you doing? Are you preparing a tray for a client?

HOPKINSON. Yes, Joan Rivers.

BURKE. *(Unimpressed.)* Oh. Is she coming over?

HOPKINSON. Any minute now. *(Coughing.)* Oh, excuse me.

BURKE. *(Moving away.)* Still with that cough? Haven't they figured it out?

HOPKINSON. Oh, it's nothing. It's more annoying than anything else, really.

(RIVERS enters.)

RIVERS. Mark! How are you?

HOPKINSON. I'm fine, Joan. I've been waiting for you. *(Turning to BURKE.)* This is Heather Burke.

RIVERS. Oh, so lovely! What a lovely face! *(Moving her hand to the young woman's face.)* But the hair, it's all wrong. It hides your features. *(Focusing her gaze on BURKE's chest.)* Oh, and you've got knockers! I've got doorbells! I stand corrected! With knockers like that, who cares about your hairstyle—even if it could use an update.

BURKE. *(Laughing politely.)* You are delightful, isn't she, Mark?

HOPKINSON. There's only one Joan!

RIVERS. Where are the jewels, Mark? When I'm depressed, and I *am* depressed, nothing lifts me up like shopping. *(To* BURKE.*)* Isn't that the case for most women? Shopping lifts our spirits the way a good surgeon can lift our faces!

BURKE. *(Laughing politely.)* Now, if you'll both excuse me, I have to get back to my department. It's been a pleasure meeting you, ma'am.

*(*BURKE *exits.)*

RIVERS. *(Looking at* BURKE *walk away.)* Such a lovely girl, but she looks frigid to me.

HOPKINSON. Joan! Please don't say that!

RIVERS. Why not? She looks like it would take a blowtorch to melt the iceberg blocking *that* vagina. *(Turning to the display tray.)* Now, these are gorgeous pieces, Mark! Absolutely gorgeous!

(A telephone rings. HOPKINSON *turns around to answer it while* RIVERS *puts on a piece of jewelry and admires herself in the mirror.)*

HOPKINSON. This is Mark. How may I help you? *(Pause.)* I see. Are you sure? What should I do? I see. *(Pause.)* Thank you.

*(*RIVERS *looks up and notices the worried expression on* BURKE*'s face.)*

RIVERS. What's wrong?

HOPKINSON. I'm not sure.

RIVERS. What do you mean you're not sure?

HOPKINSON. That was my doctor. I have walking pneumonia.

RIVERS. Walking pneumonia? *(Joking.)* That isn't anything like running diarrhea?

HOPKINSON. No, this is serious, Joan. He wants me to go back to his office to have some tests done to confirm what kind of pneumonia it is. *(Looking at her closely.)* I'm afraid, Joan. I'm afraid of what it might be.

RIVERS. Mark, can we talk? You listen to me: It will be fine. Whatever it is, *it will be fine.*

HOPKINSON. What if it isn't? What if it isn't fine?

RIVERS. If it isn't, then we can trade lives. You can be the unattractive Jewish comic whose talk show was canceled, whose husband committed suicide, whose only child refuses to speak to her, and who's so depressed she's spending what's left of her money on superfluous jewels from an overpriced shop founded by Jews who sold too cheap to a company founded by two goyim brothers from California. Is that a deal? If it isn't fine, I'll trade my miserable life for yours. *(Pause.)* Trust me, Mark, whatever it is, *it will be fine.*

Scene 4

Mark Hopkinson's apartment. Greenwich Village, New York.

RODRÍGUEZ *is tidying up, folding cloth napkins and storing them in the credenza.* HOPKINSON *walks in.*

RODRÍGUEZ. Mr. Mark, you're home early. *(Pause.)* Oh, I'm sorry, I forgot.

HOPKINSON. No offense taken, Consuelo. I forget myself at times.

RODRÍGUEZ. How long will you be...

HOPKINSON. On medical leave? I'm not sure. My doctor wants me to rest for a couple of weeks.

RODRÍGUEZ. Your pneumonia is a nasty one.

HOPKINSON. That's for sure.

RODRÍGUEZ. I told you, with my grandmother, it took almost a month before she fully recovered.

HOPKINSON. What was the treatment she received?

RODRÍGUEZ. Strong antibiotics and lots of love. I made soup for her every day.

HOPKINSON. Chicken soup?

RODRÍGUEZ. No! Turkey soup! Where my family is from, we prefer *caldo de pavo*, turkey broth soup. It's the best thing in the world when someone has a cold or the flu...

HOPKINSON. Or walking pneumonia?

RODRÍGUEZ. *Resfriados*, that's what we call any respiratory illness that's airborne. If it makes you sneeze or gives you the sniffles, then *caldo de pavo*!

(There is a pause as HOPKINSON *looks at* RODRÍGUEZ *with affection.)*

HOPKINSON. I'm glad you're a part of my life, Consuelo.

RODRÍGUEZ. Your mother? She's not talking to you still?

HOPKINSON. No, she's not. She says she loves me, but she cannot abide my lifestyle choices.

RODRÍGUEZ. I don't understand. *(Shaking her head, walking to him.)* That's something I've never been able to understand, how harsh people in this country are about judging others.

HOPKINSON. What do you mean?

RODRÍGUEZ. I don't know how to explain it. *(She struggles with her thoughts.)* In my country, we're almost all Catholic, and one of the things we are taught is that everyone has a cross to bear, challenges to overcome in their lives. If they are successful at these temptations to sin, then good. But if they are not, well, then, that's what forgiveness is about. And acceptance.

HOPKINSON. What do you mean?

(They walk over to sit down.)

RODRÍGUEZ. How can I explain it to you? *(Pause.)* Okay, look at me. We know that one of the deadly sins is Gluttony, eating too many tasty things. As you can see, I could stand to lose a few pounds, like most women. So you could say that my cross to bear is the temptation to eat too many tasty things; desserts and sweets are my downfall. Do you see? The temptation to eat sweets is *my* cross to bear! And I struggle with the urge to have an extra slice of pie, or another piece of chocolate...So, if I resist this temptation, then good for me. But often, I am weak and give in. Does that make me a bad person? No, it doesn't. It makes me one who is trying to carry this cross of fighting Gluttony with dignity and grace.

HOPKINSON. Is that how you see it?

RODRÍGUEZ. Of course! And so does everyone else! And that's how they treat me, with respect.

HOPKINSON. What do you mean?

RODRÍGUEZ. Well, my church wouldn't expel me for being chubby! I can't imagine the priest, at Mass, pointing a finger at me and saying, "Consuelo! You are guilty of the deadly sin of Gluttony! Oh, chubby one! You are hereby banished!"

HOPKINSON. *(Laughing.)* Oh, you are a delight, Consuelo.

RODRÍGUEZ. And the same applies to you, Mr. Mark.

HOPKINSON. Me? I wish I could gain a few pounds! I've been losing weight like it's out of fashion!

RODRÍGUEZ. That's not what I mean. *(Looking straight at him,* RODRÍGUEZ *takes his hand in hers.)* You know the cross *you* have to bear. It is not one of the deadly sins, but the one that is called an abomination. *That* sin.

(There is a pause.)

HOPKINSON. Abomination. That's why my mother won't speak to me.

RODRÍGUEZ. The way I see it, your...*sexual*...urges are your cross to bear. But if you give in, like I give in to that second piece of chocolate cake, it's not the end of the world. Or reason to shun someone! Because there's always forgiveness—and you can try your best tomorrow.

HOPKINSON. I'm glad you don't judge me.

RODRÍGUEZ. Mr. Mark, I'm glad my priest doesn't judge *me* when I pile on the desserts at the church holiday buffet!

*(*HOPKINSON *stands and walks to the credenza.)*

HOPKINSON. I'm also sorry that I won't be able to have you come by twice a week, Consuelo. With my medical bills and my precarious work situation...

RODRÍGUEZ. I understand, Mr. Mark.

HOPKINSON. Did the referrals I made...

RODRÍGUEZ. Oh, yes! I'm going to work Thursdays with Ms. Sharon, the woman who lives in SoHo, on Mercer Street. She lives in an old building they remodeled. It's fancy. I have to use a key in the elevator to get to her floor, and the elevator opens onto the apartment foyer! Every Thursday, her dogs are groomed and my job will be to go pick up the dogs, take them for a walk, then to the groomers. And when the three have been pampered, I'll take them home. She's divorced from her husband, she told me. And he's not allowed to come near her, she said. She has a folder with a restraining order in the kitchen, next to the drawer with the knives. If he ever rings the buzzer, she said I should call 911 and show the police those papers.

HOPKINSON. You know what that's all about, don't you?

RODRÍGUEZ. She explained it, but I didn't really understand it.

HOPKINSON. *(Walking back to her, with an envelope in his hands.)* Sharon and Greg have had a tumultuous relationship. She didn't want kids. He wanted kids. To settle the matter, they harvested her eggs and his sperm to freeze in the eventuality that they would decide to have kids. She was nearing forty, so they thought that, if it came to it, they would contract a surrogate to carry a pregnancy to term. When they divorced, the court ordered the destruction of both the eggs and sperm. I'm not sure why. But in any case, while they were married, since they had no kids, they decided to have dogs. And they have been battling over custody of the three dogs.

RODRÍGUEZ. She thinks of her dogs as if they were her children!

HOPKINSON. Exactly. That's why there's a restraining order. She has the dogs. He wants the dogs. Greg once tried to take the dogs by force. He threatened to call the SPCA on her and file a fake report about animal cruelty against her. That's when she got a restraining order.

RODRÍGUEZ. Oh, now I understand. That's why she told me that when I take the dogs out for a walk, I have to take the can of pepper spray.

HOPKINSON. Oh, I'm so sorry.

RODRÍGUEZ. Sorry about what?

HOPKINSON. Sorry that your Thursdays will involve walking dogs around SoHo armed with a can a pepper spray trying to prevent your employer's former husband from abducting those poor dogs.

RODRÍGUEZ. *(Shrugging her shoulders.)* This is how people live their lives here in New York. I'm used to it by now. I've told you that the couple I work for on Saturdays, Mr. and Mrs. Sinclair, have me cut lines of cocaine for them, since they snort cocaine before they go out for the evening. *(Rolling her eyes.)* The man of the house has six lines and the lady of the house has four. Once I tried it—they wanted me to try it. I did, but it made me sneeze! It tickled my nose. That's the fashion these days. Cocaine before going out. I think that show on television, *Miami Vice*, has made it into a fad. But I hope it's a fad that goes away soon.

(HOPKINSON *hands her the envelope as he sits down.)*

HOPKINSON. This is for you, Consuelo.

RODRÍGUEZ. What is it?

HOPKINSON. A token of my appreciation for you.

RODRÍGUEZ. *(Taking the envelope.)* You don't have to do this, Mr. Mark.

HOPKINSON. But I want to do this. You have given me more kindness than my own family. And I know you won't be getting paid as much working Thursdays for Sharon.

RODRÍGUEZ. *(Opening the envelope and counting the money.)* Ten hundred-dollar bills, Mr. Mark! That's one thousand dollars! It's too much.

HOPKINSON. No. It isn't. I wish it I could give you more. I want you to be able to pay the final semester's tuition in full. No more student debt for you, do you understand, Consuelo?

RODRÍGUEZ. Well, *muchas gracias*, Mr. Mark.

HOPKINSON. And you are welcome, my friend—*mi amiga*!

RODRÍGUEZ. Your *amiga* forever!

Scene 5

Bergdorf Goodman department store, New York.

NORTON *is assisting* BURKE *in the Bergdorf Goodman jewelry department. The two are arranging various pieces of jewelry on several trays and cleaning the glass display cases.*

NORTON. Well, I don't know what you've heard, but he is...not...doing...well...

BURKE. Is it like Rock Hudson or Perry Ellis?

NORTON. And like so many others...I heard Sylvester, that disco queen, has it. *(Whispering.)* They say Sylvester will be dead in less than a year, he's that sick. I certainly hope his tragic music dies with him! *(With disdain.)* But this dreadful disease...They still don't know how it really is spread.

BURKE. I know. Blood transfusions like that high school kid, Ryan White. Sex, like Perry Ellis. Saliva. Oh, I hope that Rock Hudson didn't endanger Linda Evans when they had that steamy kiss scene in *Dynasty*! *(Looking up.)* The truth is that no one really knows for sure.

NORTON. And Mark has been coughing all over the place. Saliva? Mucus? Snot?

BURKE. I know.

NORTON. Well, I'm just glad he's not here. And if it were up to me, he'd be in quarantine.

BURKE. I agree. I'm a little surprised at management. I mean, we've received no guidance on this thing. Is it safe to use the same restrooms? Can we trust the utensils in the café? What if he sneezes on us? It's frightening.

NORTON. It is. I think there should be quarantine.

(They look at each other.)

BURKE. Quarantine?

NORTON. I've heard that in Cuba, of all places, they are testing people, and if they have this HIV virus they are removed from the general population. Now, I'm not advocating HIV camps here...

BURKE. Can you imagine?

NORTON. I know! If we were to quarantine all the gay men with HIV...the "fabulosity" factor in this country would plummet!

(They laugh.)

BURKE. We shouldn't make light of it.

NORTON. I know, but we're talking about public health.

BURKE. And our safety!

NORTON. It breaks my heart what's going on, but no one really understands what's happening with this...

BURKE. Epidemic. AIDS is an epidemic.

NORTON. That's what it is. *(Pause.)* Did you bring the disinfectant?

BURKE. I asked, and I was told that management will not authorize it.

NORTON. Why?

BURKE. I was told it would stink up the jewelry department. They spend enough time over-thinking which flowers to put in here and each flower's scent.

NORTON. Can you imagine? They worry about clashing floral scents but don't give a damn about our well-being!

BURKE. Or our customers' well-being, for that matter.

NORTON. Well, I know they have no problem with this! *(He takes out a bottle of rubbing alcohol from his satchel.)* Mark used it to clean the mirror, so I know it won't "clash" with the aromatic ambiance of this department!

BURKE. *(Reaching for the bottle of rubbing alcohol, while* NORTON *finds a couple of small pieces of cloth.)* Give me that. Let's disinfect everything he ever touched! And we can disinfect our hands with it!

NORTON. Amen, princess! Amen to that!

*(*NORTON *and* BURKE *begin to clean feverishly the*

glass display cases, mirrors, telephone, and other objects with rubbing alcohol. They are oblivious to RIVERS *walking in.)*

RIVERS. Oh, this looks familiar! Rubbing alcohol to disinfect everything! Just like at the plastic surgeon's office!

(They look up and see RIVERS *walking over.)*

NORTON. Mrs. Rosenberg, it's a pleasure!

RIVERS. I'm here for jewelry! Not surgery! *(Pause.)* Although wouldn't it be wonderful if they could combine both? Have a facelift and a jewelry shopping splurge at the same time?

BURKE. Mrs. Rosenberg, it's good to see you.

RIVERS. *(Ignoring* BURKE.*)* I can see it now! If the wound bleeds, get a ruby necklace! If your oxygen tank runs out and you're gasping for air, then sapphires! If things are botched up and gangrene develops, then it's emeralds!

NORTON. *(Laughing.)* You are such a delightful wit!

RIVERS. Where's Mark?

NORTON. Mark is not here.

RIVERS. I can see that. Where is he?

BURKE. He's out ill.

RIVERS. Ill?

NORTON. He has some sort of pneumonia.

RIVERS. Yes, I know that. I was here last week when he found out he had walking pneumonia. That's easy to treat.

NORTON. Apparently not in his case.

RIVERS. What makes his case different? Listen to me. What makes this night different? What makes this pneumonia different? What makes this...Oh, don't get me started!

BURKE. Management told us Mark would be out for two weeks. He was diagnosed with Pneumocystis carinii pneumonia. PCP.

RIVERS. What kind of pneumonia is that?

NORTON. It's associated with people who have

suppressed immune systems.

RIVERS. Suppressed? Like Jews in the Soviet Union are suppressed?

NORTON. Yes, suppressed.

BURKE. I think that explains his weight loss.

RIVERS. You're not joking, are you?

NORTON. Why would we be?

RIVERS. As a comic, I'm used to funny things. But this isn't funny.

NORTON. I'm afraid it's not. His type of pneumonia is an opportunistic infection that attacks people with weakened immune systems.

RIVERS. Attacks?

BURKE. And we're all helping to share Mark's duties while he's out.

RIVERS. That's kind of you, especially since it's obvious to me you know nothing about precious stones.

NORTON. *(Turning to get a tray.)* And I believe this is the tray with two pieces of jewelry for you, Mrs. Rosenberg. At least that's what Mark's notes indicate.

RIVERS. Oh, you read his note? So you can read, that's a wonderful achievement. I'm sure the harpy that suckled you is very proud. *(Pause.)* Yes, those are the two rings I was considering.

(An awkward silence falls. BURKE continues to clean the glass surfaces with rubbing alcohol. RIVERS watches her.)

NORTON. These pieces are spectacular, Mrs. Rosenberg.

RIVERS. *(Addressing BURKE.)* Cleanliness is next to godliness. *(To NORTON.)* Shall I disinfect my hands with rubbing alcohol before I try on the rings?

NORTON. That won't be necessary, Mrs. Rosenberg.

RIVERS. How can you be so sure? Maybe my hands are filled with germs and viruses?

NORTON. That depends on where your hands have been, doesn't it?

(BURKE *looks at* NORTON.)

RIVERS. Do you know what?

NORTON. No, Mrs. Rosenberg, what?

RIVERS. I want to talk to a manager.

NORTON. Concerning what?

RIVERS. Concerning what? What business is it of yours?

NORTON. What I meant to say is that perhaps I can address the matter myself to your satisfaction.

RIVERS. Can we talk? I doubt it.

NORTON. Can we talk? Let's give it a try.

RIVERS. I want Mark's home telephone number. I want to talk to him.

NORTON. I'm afraid that's not possible.

RIVERS. What do you mean, that's not possible?

NORTON. Bergdorf Goodman does not disclose any employee's personal information.

RIVERS. What? You won't give me his telephone number? No, no, no, no, no. Now, you listen to me! I may not be the Joan Collins you would fawn over, but this Joan hereby demands that you give me his telephone number!

NORTON. *(Turning to* BURKE.*)* Would you please go to the office, princess?

(BURKE *exits.*)

RIVERS. Princess? What? Is there a space heater in the office so she can thaw her personality out? *(In* BURKE*'s direction.)* Ice princess!

NORTON. Mrs. Rosenberg, I hope you understand that we cannot disclose any employee's personal contact information.

RIVERS. But Mark is my friend! I want to make sure he is all right.

NORTON. *(With an attitude.)* Well, if he is your friend as you claim, then why don't you have his home telephone number? I would assume most of his friends—*if he has any*—do have his home telephone number.

RIVERS. How dare you talk back to me that way, you limp-wristed twit!

NORTON. Mrs. Rosenberg, name-calling is uncalled for!

(RIVERS *picks up a tray and smashes it on the glass display case.* NORTON *shrieks.*)

RIVERS. Now you listen to me, I repeat, you limp-wristed twit! I spit on Bergdorf Goodman's policies! After the hundreds of thousands of dollars I've squandered in this store—trying to find items that are not gaudy but tasteful—quite a tall order...You're going to treat me this way? No, no, no, no, no!

(BURKE *quickly returns and rushes to* NORTON's *side.*)

NORTON. Mrs. Rosenberg, please understand...

RIVERS. Understand? Understand what? That you won't give me Mark's telephone number? Listen, can we talk? I'm not stupid. And just because I'm short doesn't mean everything is over my head! I saw you two disinfecting everything as if it were infected with the black plague! You're afraid! You're cowards! You think Mark infected this entire department with HIV and that you can catch it by touching anything he ever touched! I've seen this before! I've seen this homophobic bigotry in action! When Perry Ellis died two years ago, his assistants were walking around his office with surgical gloves disinfecting everything as if the scissors, pincushions, measuring tapes, and everything else he ever touched was poisoned. Let me tell you something. Let me tell you what you don't want to hear but do need to hear! If you, Mr. Norton, are a gay man, then you can't turn your back and treat your ill gay brothers with disdain, as if they were pariahs, as if they were toxic. And you, Ms. Burke, if you are a fag hag—just like I'm a fag hag—then you can't turn away from the gay men who shop for shoes with you, dish the dirt with you, and tell you when you have unflattering makeup on your face. We're all in this together! All of us are in this together! Got it?

BURKE. *(Trying to calm her down.)* Of course, Mrs. Rosenberg. We haven't turned our backs on Mark. But can you blame us? Everyone is afraid of this disease—it's an epidemic.

NORTON. It's more than an epidemic; it's a pestilence.

RIVERS. Pestilence? Is that what you call it? A pestilence?

BURKE. Yes, that's what it is.

RIVERS. Oh! No, no, no, no, no! You listen to me! As long as Gwyneth Paltrow in on this earth, we will have pestilence!

BURKE. Mrs. Rosenberg, we care deeply for Mark, but we have an obligation to protect ourselves as well.

RIVERS. Don't patronize me, young woman! You can delude men with those knockers of yours, but it won't work with me! Tits do nothing for me! And let me set you straight about life: There's nothing worse in this world than a fair-weather fag hag! *(To NORTON.)* And you, Mr. Norton, remember, you can't suck on a cock without getting a little piss in your mouth now and then!

NORTON. Mrs. Rosenberg, please calm down.

BURKE. I'm afraid security will be on its way if there's a commotion.

RIVERS. Oh! Oh! Oh! Let me tell you something: Good! Let security come and they can secure you two bigots to a stockade right outside the Plaza Hotel so you can be tarred and feathered in public!

(RIVERS reaches for another tray, lifts it, and smashes it on the glass display case. NORTON shrieks. BURKE jumps back.)

NORTON. Stop! Please stop! You're causing a scene!

BURKE. Mrs. Rosenberg, please!

RIVERS. *(Mocking him.)* Stop! Please stop! You're causing a scene! *(Pointing her finger at one, then the other.)* The only way you can make me stop is to give me Mark's telephone number!

NORTON. *(Pressing the alarm button.)* Security will be here. We will press charges.

RIVERS. I don't care!

BURKE. *(Reaching for a piece of paper, jutting down a number.)* Mrs. Rosenberg, please, we can't have a commotion. We *simply* cannot have a scene on the sales floor!

NORTON. Bergdorf Goodman is not a place for a scene.

RIVERS. You may not want a scene, but that's what you're getting! *(She picks up the mirror on the glass display case and smashes it on the floor.* NORTON *shrieks.* BURKE *gasps as she recoils.)* I'm going to organize a boycott of this store! I'm going to go on television! *(To* NORTON.*)* I want the whole of New York to know you are a nothing but a self-loathing homosexual! *(To* BURKE.*)* And I want the world to see that you're nothing but a pathetic fair-weather fag hag! When I'm through with the two of you, you'll be through! *(To* NORTON.*)* You'll never suck another cock in this town again! *(To* BURKE.*)* And you, you'll never have another gay man to give you sensible fashion advice—as if you were smart enough to take it, which you obviously aren't! Don't get me started! Oh, you've *gotten* me started! And now that you've gotten me started, you better wish upon your lucky stars that you know how to finish it! Because if you don't, then I'll be the one finishing off the two of you! I spit on Bergdorf Goodman's impersonal personnel policies!

BURKE. *(Handing* RIVERS *the piece of paper.)* Mrs. Rosenberg, this is Mark's home telephone number. Please go.

NORTON. Yes, leave.

BURKE. If you leave now, we'll make up a story that we dropped the trays and set off the alarm by mistake.

NORTON. Please, leave now, Mrs. Rosenberg! Just go!

Please!

RIVERS. *(Looking at the piece of paper.)* This had better be Mark's telephone number, or the VIP room at the Chippendales strip club. If it isn't his number, I'll be back—and not with Arnold Schwarzenegger, but with a sledge hammer!

Act II

Scene 1

Mark Hopkinson's apartment. Greenwich Village, New York.

HOPKINSON, *in a bathrobe, is sitting, tired, and reading a newspaper.* RODRÍGUEZ *is moving the stacks of paper on the credenza and attending to the detritus throughout the room. Mark is about to doze off, fatigued. The telephone rings.*

HOPKINSON. Hello? *(Pause.)* You're where? Outside? Are you kidding? *(Putting down the telephone, he turns to* RODRÍGUEZ.*)* Please buzz the front door.

*(*RODRÍGUEZ *exits the room. We hear the buzzer. Then we hear the front door opening.)*

RIVERS. *(Following* RODRÍGUEZ.*)* Mark!

RODRÍGUEZ. Mr. Mark, Ms. Joan is here.

HOPKINSON. Yes, I can see. How? How did you get my number? My address?

RIVERS. Bergdorf Goodman first, then 411!

HOPKINSON. They gave you my telephone number?

RIVERS. Not management, but I persuaded a coworker to give it to me.

HOPKINSON. *(Standing to greet* RIVERS. *They kiss each other on the cheek.)* I'm so touched that you're here. Really, I didn't expect it.

RIVERS. Why wouldn't I be here? You're my friend. Besides, it isn't as if I have a husband to go home to—and Melissa isn't talking to me.

HOPKINSON. Oh, I'm sorry. I'm such a bad host. Please, have a seat, Joan.

*(*RIVERS *and* HOPKINSON *sit down.* RODRÍGUEZ *approaches.)*

RODRÍGUEZ. Would you care for anything, Ms. Joan?

RIVERS. I'm fine. Not even a glass of water—at least for now.

RODRÍGUEZ. Mr. Mark, I'm about to go to the

pharmacy for your prescriptions. Is there anything you need?

HOPKINSON. No, nothing else that I can think of, Consuelo.

RODRÍGUEZ. Mr. Mark, I prepared the solution for your enema. A colonic irrigation would do you well.

HOPKINSON. I appreciate it, Consuelo, but so many things have been up my rectum that not even a gallon of holy water would cleanse away my ass's sins!

(RODRÍGUEZ *exits.*)

RIVERS. You're a clever wit, Mark.

HOPKINSON. That's kind of you to say, but I feel anything but witty. I feel like they are treating me like Ryan White, the hemophiliac boy who became infected with HIV from a blood transfusion. Those ignorant jerks in Indiana expelled that poor youngster from middle school. Well, I feel like I've been expelled from Bergdorf Goodman. *(With sadness in his voice.)* It's something that always been a part of my life. As a boy, I understood rejection. It was terrible. Absolutely terrible. I know pain of rejection. My own father would recoil at the sight of me trying to do sports. Now I know it's because I was such a sissy growing up. But it was cruel, nonetheless. His disdain for me was terrible. He was ashamed of me, his effeminate son. I don't think I ever made him proud.

RIVERS. A parent is supposed to be there for his or her child! Always! Unconditionally!

HOPKINSON. Tell that to my parents.

RIVERS. Where are they? I mean, aren't they concerned about your health?

HOPKINSON. When I was healthy, my family was indifferent to me. *(Pause.)* But now that I'm sick, they want nothing to do with me.

RIVERS. This is terrible! What did you tell them? About getting sick? Did you lie to them? That it was a blood transfusion? *(Laughing.)* That you're Haitian?

HOPKINSON. No, nothing like that. They know I'm gay, and they hate me for it. But who's to say how I got sick? Who's to say how long I've been HIV positive? I imagine that for a lonely, closeted young man, so afraid of his parents' wrath and disapproval, the shame of it all was too much. All I know is that, arriving on the Metro-North train from Connecticut at Grand Central Station in 1976, I felt free. Walter Cronkite had just celebrated America's Bicentennial that summer. And I was so alive and young. I had turned twenty-one that spring—and I was in New York. "More, More, More" was the song that summer. Andrea True Connection was up there on the Billboard charts. *(Sings.)* "More, more, more. How do you like it? How do you like it?" *(In a serious tone.)* How did I like it? More, more, more is how I liked it! So young, everyone wanted to buy me drinks at the clubs and discos. I met Steve Rubell at a party. He told me of his grand plans to open the disco to top all discos. It was to be called Studio 54. We hung out. So you see, Joan, fabulous Jews have always been a part of my life from the first day I arrived in Manhattan!

RIVERS. You don't have to tell me about the allure of Manhattan. Steve, poor Steve Rubell—he's from Brooklyn, just like me. One of the great Brooklyn Jews who took Manhattan by storm—

HOPKINSON. He's ill, you know.

RIVERS. Is he gay? I thought he was just a cokehead and a tax cheat.

HOPKINSON. Cokehead. Tax cheat. Gay. And now he's ill. The same as me. When I found out that I was infected, I reached out to him. He confided that he's been HIV positive for three years—and that he was one of the first to get AZT. He had some way of getting it overseas or something. The FDA had not approved it for use in the U.S.

RIVERS. Steve Rubell has AIDS? Oh, oh, oh! What is going on? How can everyone be coming down with this?

HOPKINSON. Not only is Steve sick, so is Robert Mapplethorpe, whose photographs document my generation's excesses. *(Pause.)* It was the excesses of our lives that endangered us. More, more, more, that's how we liked it. More money, more alcohol, more drugs, and more sex. In my youthful innocence I thought I would find love, love at the discos, love at the bars, love at the bathhouses. But I kept looking, thinking my life would be like that Donna Summer song, "This time I know it's for real." But it wasn't. It was never for real. It was always for the moment. When the orgasm is over, so is the love. And then, in the middle of this frustrated search for love, people began to get sick. People are now desperate, for alcohol, drugs, unproven pharmaceuticals wherever they can find them. That's why Rock Hudson flew to Paris, to get treatment not available here at home. Terrible. It's all terrible. The last time I spoke with Steve, he was strung out, incoherent. His speech was slurred and he made no sense.

RIVERS. I've seen so many talented, talented, talented people destroy themselves! Oh, I don't even want to tell you.

HOPKINSON. I heard Halston is also ill, following in the steps of Perry Ellis.

RIVERS. No, no, no, no, no! I'm not going to wallow in all this talk of illness and death! You are going to be fine! There will soon be a vaccine, a cure, something! There has to be!

HOPKINSON. If Steve Rubell, with all his millions, has to smuggle AZT to double up his dosage, Joan—

RIVERS. Not another word! Let's change the subject! I've got some juicy gossip about Nancy Reagan. Oh, I suppose it isn't gossip, since she told it to me herself.

HOPKINSON. White House gossip! What is it?

RIVERS. Oh, let me tell you! Nancy—Mrs. Reagan—
can't stand Jeane Kirkpatrick, the former
ambassador to the United Nations. It turns out they
had a conflict a few years ago, and only now did she
tell me what that was all about. I had heard rumors,
but wait until you hear this, Mark! Once, when
Jeane Kirkpatrick had a meeting with President
Reagan at the White House, Jeane walks into the
Oval Office. Nancy is there and the two have it out.
Jeane calls Nancy a blow job queen—a blow job
queen! And Nancy slaps Jeane across the face!
"That's it," Mrs. Reagan said. "That bitch is out."
After that encounter she called up her astrologer in
San Francisco, that awful charlatan Joan Quigley, to
ask for advice. "When I spoke to Joan," Mrs. Reagan
told me, "she advised me that in order to maintain
an astrological balance at the United Nations, Jeane
would have to be replaced by the succeeding
astrological sign."

HOPKINSON. What? I don't understand.

RIVERS. Mark, can we talk? Astrology is fantasy! It
makes no sense, but Mrs. Reagan believes in it.

HOPKINSON. Succeeding astrological sign? What does
that mean?

RIVERS. I was confused too. So I asked Mrs. Reagan. It
turns out that Jeane Kirkpatrick is a Sagittarius.
And according to the horoscope chart, Capricorn
follows Sagittarius.

HOPKINSON. Meaning what?

RIVERS. Let me tell you! Joan Quigley advised Mrs.
Reagan that before they could fire Jeane Kirkpatrick
she would have to find a replacement who was a
Capricorn. *(Laughing.)* Can you believe that's how
our nation is run? Don't get me wrong, I love Nancy
Reagan! But she can be a dingbat!

HOPKINSON. Did they find a Capricorn to replace
Sagittarius Jeane?

RIVERS. Let me tell you! Yes, yes, yes! *(Laughing.)*

Vernon Walters is a Capricorn!

HOPKINSON. *(Laughing.)* Capricorn Vernon replaced Sagittarius Jeane to maintain astrological balance at the United Nations? *(Laughing.)* That is too ridiculous to be true!

RIVERS. Nancy Reagan. Rocks for brains!

(They pause and look at each other with affection.)

HOPKINSON. You've made me laugh, Joan.

RIVERS. And your friendship gives me faith, Mark.

HOPKINSON. I'm glad you're my "hag."

RIVERS. And I'm glad you're my "fag."

(They laugh.)

HOPKINSON. Enough about me! You're burdened with problems as well, Joan.

RIVERS. Me? My problems? No one cares about me. No one cares about my problems.

HOPKINSON. That's not true. I care.

RIVERS. Mark, Mark, Mark. At night, I cry! I cry! Why? Because I can understand that Edgar wanted to leave me! I get it. He was in pain. He was tired. He had been humiliated by Hollywood. *(Imitating a Hollywood executive.)* "Joan, baby, we love you! But you have to get rid of Edgar! He's deadweight! He's holding you back! We want you—but not if he's part of the deal!" That destroys a man's ego. That kind of talk makes a man's testicles shrivel up to nothing! So, I get why he wanted to leave me. *But he also left Melissa!* Melissa! Melissa! That beautiful baby girl we brought into this world! That bastard left *her*! He could have left me and I would have understood! But he didn't just leave *me*! That wretched bastard left *Melissa*! Our baby! And for that, I will never forgive him! I love the man, but I spit on his cowardice! He abandoned our beautiful baby girl! *(Pause.)* In the end, he disappointed me. And that's a reversal. All my life, I've disappointed men. I disappointed my father. I disappointed my husband. I've disappointed all the men in my life. And to disappoint someone is a form of betrayal. It is. It is an act of betrayal!

HOPKINSON. Is that what life has taught you?

RIVERS. Yes, it has. Life is all about betrayal. My father was a doctor, and he built a base of people he treated and cared for. People build a bond with you if you do that, take care of their health and save their lives. But me? In the entertainment industry, you are only as good as your last show, last night's ratings. That's it! There's no loyalty. And what I have found almost insurmountable is the simple truth that I'm terrible at business. I don't know business. My husband is dead. I'm vulnerable. I'm so vulnerable. No one cares about me, except for me. And I have to learn how to take care of me—so I can take care of those in my life. My daughter first and foremost—and the friends in my life, like you.

HOPKINSON. Why do you think he took his own life? I think about doing that, committing suicide if it comes to that.

RIVERS. Don't you ever, ever, ever say that again! I will slap you if you do!

HOPKINSON. *(Quietly.)* Why did Edgar kill himself?

RIVERS. I don't understand it! He was only sixty-two; he had his entire retirement ahead of him. *(Pause.)* But in all honesty, he was in pain. We weren't fighting, but we were just raw, just raw with each other. I was legally separated from him. I thought the distance would give us a chance to gather our wits about us. It wasn't about being angry at each other. It was about not being able to do the comedic act anymore—and it was affecting everything. If I couldn't make people laugh with sincerity, it affected every other aspect of my life—especially my marriage!

HOPKINSON. And Melissa? How is she?

RIVERS. Terrible. She won't speak to me. The last time we spoke it was recriminations: "I hate you! You didn't do this and you did that! You are the instigator all this! If you hadn't been separated, Daddy wouldn't have killed himself." Can you imagine dealing with this? Can you imagine? She truly thinks I could have stopped it. She thinks I was the instigator by leaving him. And we literally haven't spoken in almost a year. And all I want is for us to go into therapy together so we can resolve all this horrible, horrible, horrible anger that's eating away at her. And at me. And I am enraged at how she found out! Oh, God! Edgar overdoses in a hotel room, and they call our home. Melissa answers the telephone. "Hello, tell your mother her husband committed suicide in a hotel room." That's how she found out: Tell your *mother* that her *husband* committed suicide! Horror! Horror! Horror! That twit didn't realize she was speaking to a *daughter* whose *father* had just taken his life!

HOPKINSON. I'm so sorry about this, Joan. Especially because you are such a good person.

RIVERS. I get despondent at times, Mark. My husband is dead. Melissa isn't talking to me. I have no job to speak of. And I'm spending all my money to give myself purpose. I have no one. Except my dogs. They sit on my lap and they give me love. Other than the dogs, I have no one.

HOPKINSON. You have me.

(RIVERS *reaches over and kisses* HOPKINSON *on the forehead.)*

RIVERS. Look at the time! We've been gossiping forever! It's almost dinnertime. *(Pause.)* Which reminds me, Mark...What are you doing for dinner? Did Consuelo make something?

HOPKINSON. *(Embarrassed.)* I guess they're not here yet.

RIVERS. Who?

HOPKINSON. The service agency that delivers meals to the homebound.

RIVERS. What do you mean, they're not here yet?

HOPKINSON. Joan, I've been ruined by this disease. I'm on welfare. Consuelo is coming over once a week out of charity; I can't afford to pay her. But she insists on helping me clean the apartment. She runs errands for me. She goes to the pharmacy and buys my groceries. She does all this while juggling two jobs, two kids, and going to night school. But ever since I qualified for Social Security Disability, I'm supposed to have one warm meal delivered to me every day by that meal service agency.

RIVERS. So where is it?

HOPKINSON. The delivery drivers...sometimes...

RIVERS. Sometime what?

HOPKINSON. They skip me.

RIVERS. They skip you?

HOPKINSON. They're afraid. They're afraid of AIDS— so they forget to come by with my meal.

RIVERS. They forget you? Oh, oh, oh! No, no, no, no, no!

HOPKINSON. I can't say I blame them.

RIVERS. No, no, no, no, no! To deny someone food is to injure them! Let me tell you something: Food is what we need to survive! It is the sustenance our bodies need, and it comforts our souls. *(Pause.)* They forget you. Oh, oh, oh!

HOPKINSON. I'll be fine, Joan. Consuelo brought me boxes of cereals and those nutrition shakes.

RIVERS. No, no, no! To give someone a warm meal is to deliver God's love to them, Mark! Where's the telephone?

HOPKINSON. Over there.

RIVERS. I'm ordering dinner. *(She stands, walks over to the telephone, looks through a booklet of names and numbers. Then she dials.)* Hello? Is Elaine there? This is Joan Rivers. *(Pause.)* Ms. Kaufman, this is Mrs. Rosenberg! *Oy vey ist mir! (Laughing.)* I'm unleashing my inner Zionist, you know, and I think you should, too. I'm invoking the Talmud on you. Remember what Mishnah Sanhedrin taught: "And whoever saves a life, it is considered as if he saved an entire world." Well, here's our chance to save a life. I want you to send over some Jewish penicillin. Yes, that's right, chicken soup. Send it to me and whatever you think is good tonight. Everything's good? What? What do I want? How about an order of the veal chops and lasagna, and a couple of sides I'll leave up to you. *(Pause.)* Oh, I'm doing fine, or as fine as can be expected! Edgar, I'll never forgive his taking his own life. And Melissa, she's still not talking to me. But I have faith. Elaine, listen, I have a hungry, ill goy in desperate need of Jewish penicillin. *(Laughing.)* Yes, he still is. Mark is still my favorite *shegetz* in New York! Yes, we'll be dining in. I'm calling from his apartment. Greenwich Village, right on the corner of Bedford and Barrow. *(Pause.)* Yes, that's the place! You remembered! *(*RIVERS *hangs up and walks back to the chair to sit down.)* Dinner is on its way!

HOPKINSON. Joan, you don't have to do this. I'll be fine with a bowl of cereal, really.

RIVERS. The cereal you can save for tomorrow's breakfast, but tonight you will have a warm, nutritious meal!

HOPKINSON. Thank you, Joan.

RIVERS. I still cannot believe the meal delivery staff is afraid. There's so much ignorance about how HIV is spread, Mark. And I'll bet you're not alone. *(Pause, looking pensive.)* I remember a couple of years ago, wasn't it Jane Best and Ganga Stone who started delivering prepared meals to people living with AIDS?

HOPKINSON. I remember something about that. They were delivering meals on bicycle to the homebound.

RIVERS. That's right! Restaurant Claire, that's it! Restaurant Claire began to donate prepared meals. What's the name of their organization?

HOPKINSON. I think it's called God's Love We Deliver.

RIVERS. Tomorrow, I'm going to reach out to them, Mark. And not because you need looking after, but because delivering food to the ill is everyone's moral obligation. That's why we stay alive, to help each other. We live to take care of those who need our help, to beget the next generation of humanity, and to get them started in this world. Oh, Mark, it breaks my heart to see this cruelty. It's ignorance. It's nothing but ignorance.

(RODRÍGUEZ *enters.*)

RODRÍGUEZ. I have your prescriptions, Mr. Mark. I'll put them in your bedroom.

HOPKINSON. Thank you, Consuelo.

RIVERS. Isn't she wonderful?

(RODRÍGUEZ *returns.*)

RODRÍGUEZ. Do you need anything else?

HOPKINSON. No, I'm fine. You have a good evening, Consuelo.

RODRÍGUEZ. You too, Mr. Mark. And you also, Ms. Joan.

(RODRÍGUEZ *exits.*)

RIVERS. She's such a sweetheart, isn't she?

HOPKINSON. And so are you, Joan. It's wonderful of you to look after me.

RIVERS. Me? Oh, please. It isn't as if I had a husband waiting for me at home! Or a daughter who wanted to speak with me, either!

HOPKINSON. Oh, trust me, Joan, Melissa will come around. *(Coughing.)* You'll see.

RIVERS. Oh, oh, oh! Melissa! Melissa! Melissa! Your father is dead and there is nothing that can be done about that! But you are alive! Your mother is crying for you, my beautiful baby girl! Your mother's heart aches for you! Oh, I'd go to Temple Emanu-El on Fifth Avenue and throw myself on the floor as I recite the mourner's Kaddish for your father! But I can't. I'm not that vulgar; I'm not Bette Midler!

HOPKINSON. She will come around.

(RIVERS *and* HOPKINSON *look at each other.*)

RIVERS. Isn't life ironic? Doesn't God have a depraved sense of humor?

HOPKINSON. What do you mean?

RIVERS. What do I mean? What do I mean? Let me tell you something, Mark. Here you are, desperate to speak to your mother, and she won't have it. And here I am, dying to speak to my daughter, and she hangs up the telephone. If we could only trade places! Your mother and Melissa would be perfectly happy not saying a word to each other! And you and I, well, we'd do what we're doing now: Spending time and talking.

HOPKINSON. Life's that way, isn't it? Life is certainly full of unexpected revelations...

RIVERS. Oh, oh, oh! You want to talk about revelations? More gossip from Mrs. Reagan! Let me tell you, Mark, what is being said in certain circles: Mia Farrow is a slut! A slut, I tell you! Mrs. Reagan told me that that boy Mia Farrow had last year, Satchel, or is it Ronan? Where do they get these names? Anyway, Mrs. Reagan told me that that little boy, who'll be one year old at the end of this year, guess what? He's a *bastard*! He's a blue-eyed bastard boy!

HOPKINSON. What?

RIVERS. Oh, oh, oh! The father! Not Woody Allen, no, no, no! It's Frank Sinatra! That slut got back at Woody for screwing around with Soon-Yi Kim Chi, or whatever that Korean slut's name is, by having an affair with Ol' Blue Eyes. Have you seen the boy? Have you seen him? Mrs. Reagan was shocked: That boy has Frank Sinatra's eyes! Oh, oh, oh! Trust me! Can we talk? I love Nancy to death, but let me tell you, Mrs. Reagan has been in a position to look up and see Frank Sinatra's eyes from a certain vantage point! Frank Sinatra is certainly a mouthful!

HOPKINSON. For real?

RIVERS. Oh, grow up! Let me tell you something: If my *husband* took nude photographs of my *daughter*, and then he ran off to *marry* her, I'd also get back at that pervert by finding a handsome Hollywood star to fill up my vagina with blue-eyed sperm!

Scene 2

Bergdorf Goodman department store, New York.

NORTON *is on the telephone.*

> NORTON. Princess, Mrs. Rosenberg just called. She's
> around the corner. She is coming by to pick up those
> Perry Ellis shirts for Mark. *(Pause.)* I know! She
> goes over to his apartment. *(Pause.)* I wouldn't. Who
> knows what viruses are floating about in his home?
> *(Pause.)* I agree, I agree with you on that point. But
> anyway, just come down so we can get her out of
> here without delay.
>
> (RIVERS *enters, walking directly to* NORTON. NORTON
> *hangs up the telephone and, looking up, sees her.*
> RIVERS *approaches, extending her hand to him. He
> recoils, removes the handkerchief in his breast
> pocket, and brings it to his mouth).*
>
> RIVERS. Are you about to sneeze, Mr. Norton? Or do
> you have unwanted pubic hair between your teeth?
>
> NORTON. *(Deadpan.)* Neither, Mrs. Rosenberg.
> *(Lying.)* I'm afraid I might be coming down with a
> cold and I don't want to spread my germs, especially
> since I know you will be going to Mark's apartment
> from here...and his health is...shall we say,
> precarious?
>
> RIVERS. A cold? In July?
>
> NORTON. Summer colds have been known to happen,
> Mrs. Rosenberg.
>
> RIVERS. Are they anything like hot flashes? I would
> suspect you are familiar with the sensation of hot
> flashes rushing through your loins.
>
> (BURKE *enters. She is wearing blue surgical gloves, a
> blue surgical mask, and is holding a lavender
> Bergdorf Goodman shopping bag in front of her as if
> had a dead skunk.)*
>
> NORTON. *(Ignoring* RIVERS*).* Oh, Heather, you are a

princess. *(To* RIVERS.*)* Here are the items Mark requested, Mrs. Rosenberg.

*(*RIVERS *looks at* NORTON *and* BURKE. RIVERS *seethes with anger.)*

RIVERS. Oh, oh, oh! No, no, no, no, no! I'm not letting you get away with this behavior. *(Grabbing the shopping bag, to* BURKE.*)* Give me that, you fair-weather fag hag. *(Pointing her finger at the both* NORTON *and* BURKE.*)* Now you listen to me! How dare you act this way! A handkerchief over your mouth! A surgical mask! What's the matter with you? None of this has any basis in science! I understand there's widespread fear and ignorance about HIV and AIDS. But you, Mr. Norton, with a handkerchief over your mouth, and you, Ms. Burke, with surgical gloves! You are both ridiculous! There is no scientific evidence to suggest that HIV is transmitted through casual contact—and you are both guilty of AIDS phobia. Do you think Mark should be in quarantine? Do you think there should be a patrol car outside his apartment building to make sure he doesn't leave? Do you think there should be a ban on travel by people living with AIDS? Shame on both of you! And if you're going to act this way—you might as well move to New Jersey!

*(*RIVERS *takes the bag and exits in a huff.* NORTON *and* BURKE *look at each other.* NORTON *turns around, grabs the bottle of rubbing alcohol, pours some into his handkerchief, and wipes his face and hands.)*

NORTON. Want some?

BURKE. Desperately!

*(*NORTON *hands her the bottle.* BURKE *takes off her surgical gloves and surgical mask. She wipes alcohol all over her hands.)*

NORTON. Help me wipe down the glass.

BURKE. Can you believe that woman? She's a walking petri dish of diseases!

Scene 3

Mark Hopkinson's apartment. Greenwich Village, New York.

HOPKINSON *is sitting down.* RIVERS *lets herself in with her own set of keys.*

> RIVERS. *(Handing* HOPKINSON *the Bergdorf Goodman shopping bag.)* Here are the Perry Ellis shirts you wanted, Mark.
>
> HOPKINSON. Oh, thank you. How are Dale and Heather?
>
> RIVERS. *(Lying.)* They're charming as ever. And they send their regards. They are anxious for you to get healthy and return to work.
>
> HOPKINSON. *(Taking one shirt out of the bag, he picks up a pair of tiny scissors and begins to cut loose the label on the inside of the shirt collar that reads "Perry Ellis.")* Oh, I hope I get better and can return to work. I have to say that the happiest times in my life have been at Bergdorf Goodman. I love that store. It's more than a place to buy things.
>
> RIVERS. You are right about that. Bergdorf Goodman is a temple. It is a sacred place where one's emotional needs are satisfied.
>
> HOPKINSON. *(Sewing the Perry Ellis label onto a piece of lavender silk cloth.)* It's like that disco song by Sylvester, "Make me feel mighty real!" Working at Bergdorf Goodman makes me feel mighty real—and *alive.* I love the customers! I love the exquisite merchandise! I love the energy of being on Fifth Avenue steps away from the Plaza Hotel and Central Park. It makes me feel mighty real. *(Singing softly.)* "Make me feel mighty real."
>
> RIVERS. Enough nostalgia! Please! You're still alive! *(Laughing.)* You're still mighty real!
>
> HOPKINSON. *(Standing up, coughing slightly.)* Here, Joan. Help me with this.

(HOPKINSON *extends the piece of cloth, the size of a panel for the NAMES AIDS Memorial Quilt.* RIVERS *stands and holds one end up.*)

RIVERS. What is this?

HOPKINSON. For the NAMES project. I thought Perry Ellis should have a quilt. And I thought that his own label would be enough of a tribute to him. Lavender, the color of our community.

RIVERS. It's beautiful. It is a moving tribute to Perry Ellis, Mark.

(HOPKINSON *and* RIVERS *begin to fold the piece of cloth.*)

HOPKINSON. I don't think anyone made a quilt for him. (HOPKINSON *takes the folded panel and walks to the sideboard, where there is a large yellow padded envelope.*) I'm going to mail it to the NAMES AIDS Memorial project.

RIVERS. That's a very dear thing, Mark. Very, very dear of you.

(HOPKINSON *pauses and turns around to face* RIVERS.)

HOPKINSON. Will you promise me one thing, Joan?

RIVERS. What?

HOPKINSON. That when the time comes...That when my time comes, that you'll make a quilt for me?

RIVERS. (*Walking over to him, she embraces him as he cries.*) Oh, Mark, Mark, Mark! Everything is going to be fine! I'm almost a quarter century older than you! You're the one who's going to be coming to place flowers—red roses, I insist—on my grave! You're going to live long enough to be at my funeral.

HOPKINSON. (*Slowly.*) It's kind of you to say that, but no, I won't. I'm not going to survive this!

Scene 4

Bergdorf Goodman department store, New York.

NORTON *stands at the glass display case.* RIVERS *enters.*

RIVERS. Good afternoon, Mr. Norton. I'm here to pick up Mark's personal things.

NORTON. *(Reaching for a small cardboard box.)* It's a good thing you came over this afternoon, Mrs. Rosenberg. Another day and it would have been sent to be incinerated.

RIVERS. Incinerated?

NORTON. Of course. Isn't that the standard procedure for biohazards?

RIVERS. *(Putting her purse on the glass case, she opens it.)* Mark has a note for you and Heather. It's in here. *(Removing items from her purse, deliberately spreading them all over the glass display case to annoy* NORTON.*)*

NORTON. *(Noticing three photographs that spilled out, reaching for them.)* Mrs. Rosenberg? Why do you have photographs of Queen Elizabeth, Paloma Picasso, and Sarah Jessica Parker in your purse?

RIVERS. Confidence.

NORTON. Confidence?

RIVERS. Yes, it's for my confidence?

NORTON. I don't understand.

RIVERS. It's important to remind myself that there are at least three women in the world that are uglier than me!

NORTON. Yes, of course. But that still puts you in the Top Ten of ugliest women on earth.

RIVERS. True, but better than being the gold, silver, and bronze medalists of ugliness. *(Pause.)* Let's face it. These three women look like horses! They could be the mares in Mr. Ed's harem!

NORTON. That's unkind of you to say.

RIVERS. As if you knew anything about kindness, Mr. Norton. *(She finds the note and puts things back in her purse, taking the photograph of Paloma Picasso from* NORTON'S *hand.)* Now, Mr. Norton, I ask you: What's the difference between Paloma Picasso and a Spanish drag queen?

NORTON. What?

RIVERS. See? You don't know, either!

NORTON. That's not funny.

RIVERS. It is if you hum it.

NORTON. You're hard to stand. No wonder your husband committed suicide.

RIVERS. *(In a stern manner.)* Mr. Norton, I know that every time you see me you wish I were Joan Collins. But let me tell you something. If Joan Collins looks better than I do, it is only because *her* pact with Satan is tighter than mine! *(Taking the box of* HOPKINSON'S *belongings, she hands the note to* NORTON.) This note is for you and Heather, you limp-wristed twit!

NORTON. Mrs. Rosenberg, I'd like to show you something.

RIVERS. What?

NORTON. *(Pointing to the entrance.)* The exit.

Scene 5

Mark Hopkinson's apartment. Greenwich Village, New York.

RODRÍGUEZ *is tidying up the living room when* RIVERS *walks in. The women converse as they both tidy up the place.*

> RODRÍGUEZ. I worry so much about Mr. Mark. I know he's trying his best, but I just think it would be better for him if his mother or sister were here!
>
> RIVERS. What do you mean?
>
> RODRÍGUEZ. It's just that when someone is ill...Well, there's nothing like having the love of family to lift your spirits and give you courage!
>
> RIVERS. I agree with you, Consuelo.
>
> RODRÍGUEZ. *(Reaching for bonbons and eating one.)* I'm sorry. I don't mean to be a glutton. It just that when I get nervous, I overeat. *(Pause.)* You know that sweets are my cross to bear, Ms. Joan. *(Offering her the plate with bonbons.* RIVERS *takes one.)* I just eat and eat! It's the deadly sin of Gluttony, I know, and I need to learn to resist these temptations. But I can't. When I'm nervous, I just eat!
>
> RIVERS. These are good!
>
> RODRÍGUEZ. They're from Balducci's. My friend works there and gets the employee discount. *(Pause.)* It's good, but it's bad. I can afford them, but I can't afford to eat them!
>
> RIVERS. You're funny, Consuelo. "I can afford them, but I can't afford to eat them." I could use that in a stand- up.
>
> RODRÍGUEZ. Take it, it's yours.
>
> RIVERS. *(Reaching for the bonbons.)* I'd rather take these bonbons.
>
> RODRÍGUEZ. *(Watching* RIVERS *eat a couple of chocolates.)* You really like them, Ms. Joan. That's good.
>
> RIVERS. Even if they were awful, I'd still be eating

them. Let me tell you something, Consuelo. In my life, when I'm depressed, I eat. All you have to do is look at a photograph of me. If I'm thin, then that's because things are going well in my life and I'm happy. If I'm chubby, then I'm depressed. Ever since my dear husband committed suicide, I've been gaining weight. One pound last month, two pounds the next, another pound the following month. It's terrible.

RODRÍGUEZ. Is the deadly sin of Gluttony your cross to bear also?

RIVERS. Cross to bear? What?

RODRÍGUEZ. Yes, the temptation you spend a lifetime trying to resist. Your cross to bear.

RIVERS. Oh, oh, oh! No, no, no, no, no! I'm a Jew. Jews don't bear crosses—except for that one time one of us bore a cross—and he ended up crucified to it!

(HOPKINSON *enters.*)

RODRÍGUEZ. Mr. Mark, you're up from your nap so soon?

HOPKINSON. I just couldn't sleep.

RODRÍGUEZ. Are you still having nightmares?

HOPKINSON. Yes, and it's the same one over and over again.

RIVERS. Is it the one in which you are all alone?

HOPKINSON. Yes.

RODRÍGUEZ. It's because no one from Bergdorf Goodman has come by to visit, isn't it?

HOPKINSON. I can't blame them. Yes, I know they are imposing this cruel ostracism on me, but it is out of fear, not hatred. *(Pause.)* It still stings. I can understand strangers who are afraid to deliver dinner to me, but when friends keep their distance in this manner, it is almost too much. That's why I appreciate your being here, Joan—and I appreciate you, Consuelo, who remain steadfast in your friendship. And indifferent to the social stigma of this wretched disease.

RODRÍGUEZ. Let me make some tea for all of us, Mr. Mark.

(RODRÍGUEZ exits.)

RIVERS. You can't blame yourself, Mark. (RIVERS *takes a seat, as does* HOPKINSON.*)* The world is full of frightened cowards, that's all.

HOPKINSON. Why? Why did I get this? *(Crying.)* What did I do? It was my fault.

RIVERS. Mark, this is a disease, not a moral judgment!

HOPKINSON. At times I blame the promiscuity that's been part of my life, willing to spend the cash in my pocket as easily as I was willing to spend the night with someone whose name I never even cared to ask. And here you are, my friend. And here is Consuelo, looking after me. Without a moralistic tone, Consuelo is there, present as a saint watching over me. But she knows. She knows there will come a day, too soon, when we will say a final farewell. Her life will continue; mine will end. She will be left to sweep up the mess I'm leaving behind.

RIVERS. Don't say things like that, Mark.

HOPKINSON. But it's the truth. There is spectacle in my demise, but only because I am young and my death will be "tragic." That's a different kind of tragedy from the death of an older person, someone who's lived out his natural life. I feel as alone as Liberace at the end. Oh, how I cried last year when he died! My mother also cried. That was the only time when my mother acted with compassion toward anything that had to do with AIDS. "I know he was far from perfect," she said, which is her way of saying "gay." In my family, if you're far from perfect, then you're gay or lesbian, or some other kind of disappointment to your family. But in Liberace's case, she asked what *I* have asked of *my* fate: *Why?* "Why did he have to get that dreadful thing? He was such a nice man, not some hustler or pervert, drug addict or depraved creature." To her way of thinking it was almost as shocking as when Rock Hudson, that all-American movie star, admitted he was sick. *(Pause.)* That's like my mother; she spent all her compassion on strangers, leaving none for me.

RIVERS. We're here for you, Mark. You're not alone.

HOPKINSON. I know that, but I can't help but think I brought this upon myself. All my excesses! More, more, more? That's how I liked it! And I'll tell you something: That's how I got infected!

RIVERS. *(With levity.)* More, more, more! Oh, God of Abraham! That should be the national anthem of Israel!

HOPKINSON. Please don't make me laugh!

RIVERS. *(With levity.)* Let me tell you a vulgar joke— which means I'll tell you a Bette Midler joke!

HOPKINSON. Stop!

RIVERS. *(Imitating Bette Midler.)* I was in bed last night with my boyfriend, Ernie. And he said to me, "Soph, you got no tits and your box is tight." I said to him, "Ernie, get off my back!"

HOPKINSON. *(Laughing through his tears.)* Stop! *(Pause.)* I remember when I'd go see her at the Continental Baths at the Ansonia Hotel. She was great, this crass woman telling tawdry jokes at a gay bathhouse.

RIVERS. Good for her! A gig is a gig. And a gig is money!

HOPKINSON. She was a riot!

RIVERS. Let me tell you something, Mark. Can we talk? The only thing worse than a *vulgar* Jew is a *penniless* Jew!

HOPKINSON. You are incorrigible!

RIVERS. I have something to tell you...

HOPKINSON. What?

RIVERS. Melissa called me!

HOPKINSON. *(Excited.)* She did?

RIVERS. Yes! My baby girl and I are going to go to therapy and talk out all the issues—her father's suicide, her complaints about me, everything, everything, everything!

HOPKINSON. Oh, Joan, that makes me so very happy! At least one of my prayers has been answered!

RIVERS. May *all* your prayers be answered!

Scene 6

Bergdorf Goodman department store, New York.

BURKE *stands at the glass display case.* RIVERS *walks in.*

RIVERS. Where's Dale?

BURKE. He's sick.

RIVERS. Oh?

BURKE. That blotch on his skin. It turned out it is *Karposi sarcoma.* That's the gay cancer.

RIVERS. *(Stunned.)* Oh, I am very, very, very sorry to hear that.

BURKE. It's awful, Mrs. Rosenberg. It's just awful. *(With sorrow.)* He's going to die—just like the rest of them. Everyone who gets that cancer dies from it!

(RIVERS *reaches for* BURKE*'s hand.* BURKE *cries.)*

RIVERS. It took this to melt the iceberg!

BURKE. What?

RIVERS. Nothing, nothing, my child. *(Pause.)* We have got to do something about this! We have got to fight this epidemic!

BURKE. It's terrifying, Mrs. Rosenberg.

RIVERS. Let me tell you something, Ms. Burke. In life, you have to stay strong! Always! And as the strong woman that you are, I expect you to get a grip.

BURKE. Yes, I understand.

RIVERS. Good! That's how it has to be! Every woman has to be strong if she's to get by in this world.

BURKE. *(Getting herself together.)* Are you here for a specific item, Mrs. Rosenberg?

RIVERS. I'm not here to shop. *(Pause.)* I have bad news and I wanted to let you—and Bergdorf Goodman management—know in person, not by telephone.

BURKE. What?

RIVERS. Mark has taken a turn for the worse.

BURKE. Oh, no. How worse?

RIVERS. It is horrible, horrible, horrible. He was

hospitalized two days ago. Multiple infections, high fever, dehydration.

BURKE. Oh, Mrs. Rosenberg, no. What do the doctors say?

RIVERS. The doctors say he has a few days left, if not hours. He's slipping in and out consciousness. The fever is frying his brain.

BURKE. Dear Mark!

RIVERS. Yes, it's dreadful. But Mark, being meticulous, planned his own memorial service.

BURKE. He did?

RIVERS. Yes. The third Sunday next month we will gather to celebrate his life. No one expects his family to make an appearance, but it would be wonderful if his friends and colleagues at Bergdorf Goodman showed up.

BURKE. Of course. I understand completely.

RIVERS. Good. After his end comes—in the next few days—a program will be printed with the final details about the memorial service. I'll bring invitations for you and everyone here.

BURKE. Yes, please do, Mrs. Rosenberg!

RIVERS. The things that happen in this world, Ms. Burke! That's why you have to be a strong woman! This world isn't for sissies!

Scene 7

Mark Hopkinson's apartment. Greenwich Village, New York.

RODRÍGUEZ *is sitting down, sewing. There are boxes stacked everywhere. Yellow notes are taped some pieces of furniture and a few other items. The buzzer rings.* RODRÍGUEZ *puts down her sewing on the occasional coffee table and stands to answer the door. She returns accompanied by* RIVERS.

>
> RIVERS *(Looking around, gesticulating.)* Oh, oh, oh! Don't tell me that it is all being packed away.
>
> RODRÍGUEZ. Mr. Mark's family doesn't want anything.
>
> RIVERS. But why? It's gorgeous! Art Deco furniture, exquisite. It's all exquisite.
>
> RODRÍGUEZ. His family doesn't want anything that will remind them of him. His sister was here two days ago. She took his watches, gold cuff links, anything of value. She also took all the legal papers, insurance policies, bank statements, and a few family photographs. Then three people from Sotheby's arrived as she was about to leave. They examined every single piece of furniture and they put those tags on what is going to be sold at auction.
>
> RIVERS. And the rest? *(Walking to the framed photographs on the wall of movie stars and print advertising.)* What's to become of the rest of his belongings?
>
> RODRÍGUEZ. Mr. Mark's sister told me I could take whatever I wanted to keep as mementos. The rest is to be donated to Goodwill Industries. They are coming tomorrow. She told me to be sure to get a receipt for tax purposes.
>
> RIVERS. *(Looking at the furnishings as she walks to the chairs.)* And so it will end this way, Mark's time in this world.
>
> RODRÍGUEZ. And there's a rush to empty the

apartment. I was told that next week the management wants everything out. They are eager to paint, update the kitchen, and remodel the bathroom. The super told me they are going to quadruple the rent—that's how long Mr. Mark lived here, with rent control.

RIVERS. "It's all about the money, honey." *(Sitting down.)* That's what Andy Warhol always used to say when someone died. It's all about the money, honey.

RODRÍGUEZ. For the building owners, yes. But for Mr. Mark's family? I don't think they care. Some of the things they are donating are valuable. *(Standing to walk over to the stacked boxes.)* But when I mentioned it to his sister, she shook her head. *(Pointing to various items as she speaks.)* "No," she told me. "Neither my mother nor I want any of this queer stuff. It's all disgusting. Why would we want Erté prints? Or a collection of Ethel Merman albums? Those framed photographs of Madonna? Or revolting pornographic books from that Tom of wherever in Scandinavia? No, absolutely not! We have no use for any of this, nor do we wish to introduce this filth into our homes. My brother was so lost in all of this...all of this...*perversion.* May God forgive the depravity of his soul."

RIVERS. She said that? Oh, oh, oh! It's a good thing I wasn't here or I would have put that homophobic wretch in her place!

RODRÍGUEZ. *(Sitting down, she continues her sewing.)* Mr. Mark was always shunned by his family. It made me sad. His mother never invited him over to her house for Thanksgiving. His sister always had an excuse why he couldn't go over for Christmas. He told me he had only seen his two nephews and his niece three times. And the oldest one turned twelve this year.

RIVERS. That breaks my heart. In the end, family is all we have. Family is all that matters. *(Pause.)* That makes me so depressed, I need a piece of chocolate.

RODRÍGUEZ. (*Putting down the quilt, she reaches for a box of bonbons.*) Here, have the rest.

RIVERS. (*Taking a chocolate.*) This is just so wrong, the bigotry, the rejection. Let me tell you something about this country. We all pretend we're Americans and that we are united and stand up for each other, but that's not true. We are a country torn apart by hatred. Everyone wants to talk about "tolerance." Tolerance for this and tolerance for that. Let me tell you what tolerance means. It means to put up with something. It means to suffer in silence. It doesn't mean that you like something or someone. It just means that you learn to grin, bear it, and not say a word while you seethe in silence! That's what tolerance in America is all about.

RODRÍGUEZ. (*Eating a bonbon and then returning to her sewing.*) I don't understand. I thought being tolerant is a good thing.

RIVERS. Don't get me started! Tolerance is to put up with something you can't stand. It's passive-aggressive. Let me tell you something. This country hates Jews. It just does. And the only way that we Jews have been able to succeed is to disguise our true identities. Rivers is a Christian name—but I had to adopt a Christian name because if I went out there in this country with a Jewish name, I would have encountered many, many, many more obstacles than I have for being a woman, for being brash.

RODRÍGUEZ. Rivers is not your name?

RIVERS. Of course not! My father's name was Molinsky. I am Joan Alexandra Molinsky. But when I began to have some success, my agent, Tony Rivers, told me I had to change my name. "To what?" I asked. "To something Christian," he said. I was so furious I couldn't even think. So I said, "Fine, I'll take your name, you stupid goy!" And that's how I became Joan Rivers. Do you think America would have been interested in *The Late Show Starring Joan Molinsky*? Of course not. Even my married

name was unacceptable: Rosenberg. *The Late Show
Starring Joan Rosenberg* would never have been
aired. The discrimination Jews faced was un-
Christian!

RODRÍGUEZ. I didn't know that.

RIVERS. And I wasn't alone. My dear friend and
colleague, another female Jewish comic, was Totie
Fields. She was born Sophie Feldman. But in this
country, there might be tolerance for a *female* comic,
but there wouldn't be success for a female comic
named *Feldman*. And she wanted to be successful.
So Feldman became Fields. Larry King was born
Larry Zeiger, Kirk Douglas was born Isadore
Demsky, Milton Berle was born Milton Berlinger,
Woody Allen was born Allen Konigsberg, Jerry
Lewis was born Joseph Levitch, Tony Curtis was
born Bernard Schwartz, and Tony Randall was born
Arthur Rosenberg. The list is endless. We all had to
change our names to disguise the truth that we were
Jews! *(She takes another bonbon.)* Let me tell you
something: You tolerate a toothache until you get
yourself to the dentist. Hundreds of Jews had to take
Christian names in Hollywood if they wanted to be
tolerated—and successful. To think we had to hide
our true identities to be successful! It makes me
seethe! Oh, let me tell you. Can we talk? Growing
up, I was among the Jewish youngsters who were
taunted by school kids, "Christ killer! Christ Killer."
It's easy to laugh it off, but, as a child, it wounds
your spirit, and it makes you feel like you're always
an outsider. I spit on this Christian nation's
bigotries! And I detest Jews who ignore this history
and pretend that anti-Semitism is a thing of the
past. Take Ed Koch—that closet case! Oh, I spit on
his refusal to acknowledge the historic
discrimination against Jews in New York, and I spit
on his refusal to declare his sexuality! He could be
such an example to so many who are afraid to be
themselves, to live their lives with honesty and

integrity! Here's a good one about our mayor! *(Pause for dramatic effect.)* What's the difference between Ed Koch and a Rolls Royce? *(Slight pause.)* More people have been in Ed Koch! *(Laughs, then catches her breath.)* That's why I will never shut up about the right of people to be proud of who they are—how God made them! Let me tell you something, Consuelo. Two years ago, when I hosted a benefit for AIDS, I couldn't get one major star to turn out. It was horrible! The shame and the prejudice that existed is still enormous. And that's the hurt and sense of being outsiders that gays, lesbians, and transgender people feel. That's how it is with AIDS! It took Rock Hudson's admission to change that. Rock's admission was a horrendous way to bring AIDS to the attention of the American public, but by so doing Rock, in his life, has helped millions in the process. What Rock did took true courage.

RODRÍGUEZ. Mr. Mark had a framed photograph of Rock Hudson in his bathroom.

RIVERS. *(Laughing.)* Not a picture of me? But in all seriousness, let me tell you something. The same prejudice takes place with Hispanics today. You have to adopt Anglo names if you want to be successful.

RODRÍGUEZ. Really?

RIVERS. Oh! Of course! Do you think Martin Sheen was born Martin Sheen? Of course not! His driver's license says Ramón Estévez. I've seen it. Do you think Raquel Welch was born Raquel Welch? Of course not! Her birth certificate says "Raquel Tejada." Although with knockers like hers, it doesn't matter what's on her birth certificate! She was bound to be successful! Let me tell you, if I had knockers like hers, I'd be the president of the United States! Estévez and Tejada were born to be actors, but they could only be *successful* actors if they adopted an Anglo identity. So, Consuelo, remember. In this country, if you want to be yourself, then you have to hide who you are!

RODRÍGUEZ. Are you sure, Ms. Joan? I say this because Mr. Mark spent so many years trying to hide who he was, and look where that got him. I told him he should never have been ashamed of who he is, because that's how God made him.

RIVERS. In Utopia that works, but in my business? That's not how corporate America works. There's no loyalty, Consuelo. Fox dropped me without a second thought. Bergdorf Goodman turned its corporate back on Mark without a moment's hesitation.

RODRÍGUEZ. I'm sorry this is the way things are—

RIVERS. But only for Jews, Hispanics, blacks, gays, lesbians, Muslims, Chinese, Japanese, Native Americans, Buddhists, Catholics, Eastern Europeans, the left-handed...

RODRÍGUEZ. *(Laughing.)* Have another bonbon, Ms. Joan.

RIVERS. How about another dozen? *(Pause.)* I think you should change your name, Consuelo.

RODRÍGUEZ. Why? I love my name.

RIVERS. *(Looking up.)* Consuelo should become... *Constance*. And Rodríguez should be... *Rodham*. *Consuelo Rodríguez* will never be as successful as *Constance Rodham*. A medical assistant named Constance Rodham will be promoted to supervisor *decades* before a medical assistant named Consuelo Rodríguez gets the same promotion!

RODRÍGUEZ. What? What are you saying?

RIVERS. Let me tell you something, *Constance*. Every time I meet a "José," I tell him to drop the "s." *Joe Garcia* will have a career. *José García* will be washing dishes for the rest of his life!

RODRÍGUEZ. I don't think surrendering your identity will lead to happiness, do you?

RIVERS. Was he happy?

RODRÍGUEZ. Who?

RIVERS. Mark. Was he happy? I mean, where was he the happiest?

RODRÍGUEZ. Mr. Mark always told me that he was happiest at Bergdorf Goodman. He told me that no one judged him there. All they cared about was that he was a good salesman who treated the customers properly.

RIVERS. That's what he also told me. Bergdorf Goodman gave him the kind of happiness no one in his family did. Do you see what I mean about tolerance? Mark's family tolerated him, but they didn't accept him. *(Rolling her eyes.)* "This is my homosexual son." *(Rolling her eyes.)* "This is my cocksucker of a brother." Only his friends—his chosen family—loved him.

RODRÍGUEZ. That includes us, Ms. Rodríguez and Ms. Rivers.

RIVERS. Mrs. Rosenberg.

RODRÍGUEZ. Mrs. Rosenberg?

RIVERS. That's my married man. When Edgar committed suicide, we were legally separated, but we were still married.

RODRÍGUEZ. Suicide?

RIVERS. Yes, he overdosed on prescription medications.

RODRÍGUEZ. *(Making the sign of the cross.)* Suicide. That's the most selfish thing a person can do.

RIVERS. Selfish? Why do you say that, Consuelo?

RODRÍGUEZ. Because the suicide has the final word.

RIVERS. *(Laughing.)* In Edgar's case, the shmuck left a videotaped suicide message! He *did* have the final word—and videotape to go along with it. He was a schmuck, but I loved that schmuck with all my heart!

RODRÍGUEZ. *(Sighing, she unfurls the quilt.)* Bueno, Mr. Mark's quilt is done.

RIVERS. *(Standing up and reaching for an end of the quilt to extend it fully.)* Gorgeous! Gorgeous! Didn't I tell you it needed those red sequins?

RODRÍGUEZ. You were right, Ms. Joan. I thought it might look too gaudy, but it's tasteful.

RIVERS. It's gorgeous. And the fabric with the Bergdorf Goodman logo is absolutely fabulous. *(RIVERS stands and walks to the onyx sideboard buffet.)* What's with this gorgeous piece of furniture?

RODRÍGUEZ. Oh, that? The woman from Sotheby's said it was worth almost $20,000 at auction. She said that Art Deco and anything from the Mid-Century Modern are the next big waves in desirable furnishings. I'm not sure what she meant, but Mr. Mark's sister became very excited when she heard that.

RIVERS. *(Looking over the furniture, she notices a box.)* What is this?

RODRÍGUEZ. Mr. Mark.

RIVERS. *(Surprised.)* What?

RODRÍGUEZ. *(Making a sign of the cross.)* Those are his ashes.

RIVERS. What are they doing here?

RODRÍGUEZ. Mr. Mark's mother refused to accept them. She told them to send them here.

RIVERS. What does his sister say?

RODRÍGUEZ. She says she doesn't know what to do with them. She was going to think about it. Then she said something as a joke, but I didn't know what to think.

RIVERS. What?

RODRÍGUEZ. That if she couldn't figure out what to do, she'd just flush them down the toilet when she came back next week to hand in the keys and sign off on the apartment.

RIVERS. Oh! Oh! Oh! No, no, no, no, no! Let me tell you something: That is not going to happen. *(Pause.)* Mark Hopkinson belongs to be where he was the happiest!

RODRÍGUEZ. What do you mean?

RIVERS. *(Taking the box, briskly walking to get her satchel.)* What I mean is that I'm going to spread his ashes where they should be spread, Consuelo.

RODRÍGUEZ. Ms. Joan, you're not going to do what I think you're going to do!

RIVERS. Yes, I am! You bet I am! This is the last thing that I can do for my friend!

RODRÍGUEZ. You won't get in trouble?

RIVERS. Consuelo, finish the last details on the quilt. I'll be back later this afternoon. We can then take the quilt and we will both, *together*, mail it to Cleve Jones at the NAMES AIDS Memorial Quilt.

(RIVERS picks up her satchel, walks over to kiss RODRÍGUEZ on the cheek. She grabs one more bonbon and rushes out. RODRÍGUEZ shakes her head and returns to finish sewing the edge of the quilt.)

RODRÍGUEZ. I pray to the Virgin Mary that Ms. Joan doesn't end up on the evening news!

Scene 8

Bergdorf Goodman department store, New York.

RIVERS *nonchalantly walks into the jewelry department as usual, but she scrutinizes the place with a newfound intensity.* BURKE *is arranging some items in a jewelry case. She approaches* BURKE.

> RIVERS. Good afternoon.
>
> BURKE. *(With enthusiasm.)* Mrs. Rosenberg! It's a pleasure to see you.
>
> *(The women exchange "air" kisses as each leans over the glass display case.)*
>
> RIVERS. How are you doing since—
>
> BURKE. I do miss Dale very much, and it is all very sad. They say he will be on permanent disability because his cancer has spread. *(Pause.)* But what happened to Mark—that is even more tragic.
>
> RIVERS. It's awful, just awful what is happening. But that's why I'm here, to lift my spirits with a little shopping!
>
> BURKE. And we have received the most beautiful items, Mrs. Rosenberg.
>
> RIVERS. Where are they?
>
> BURKE. In the safe. In the back.
>
> RIVERS. Can you get them?
>
> BURKE. *(Whispering.)* I'm not sure we're supposed to be showing them before next week. Much excitement about the new fall collection.
>
> RIVERS. *(Conspiratorially.)* I won't tell anyone. It will be our little secret. Will you go get them? I have a little time. I can wait.
>
> BURKE. Perfect, Mrs. Rosenberg. I'll be no more than a couple of minutes!
>
> RIVERS. Oh, oh, oh! Take your time, Ms. Burke! Don't rush back!
>
> *(*BURKE *exits.* RIVERS *is alone.* RIVERS *looks around*

and puts her satchel on the glass display case. She takes out the box of ashes. She begins to walk around the jewelry department and surreptitiously scatters the ashes as if they were talcum powder. She scatters them on the carpets, on the glass display cases, by the walls, and in the corners. When she is done, she returns to her spot to wait for BURKE. *She sprinkles the last of the ashes around the glass display case and wipes her hands clean.* BURKE *returns.)*

BURKE. *(Holding a tray in her hands.)* Here they are, Mrs. Rosenberg!

RIVERS. Gorgeous! Gorgeous! Gorgeous! *(She reaches to touch them.)* I think I want them! Will you set them aside? *(*BURKE *turns to get a notepad.)* Oh, oh, oh! Look at the time! I just remembered that I'm late to meet a friend at Elaine's. You have my information, just set them aside! Gorgeous! Absolutely gorgeous!

BURKE. *(Turning around.)* Of course, Mrs. Rosenberg.

RIVERS. Sorry that I have to run off like this! *(*RIVERS *quickly tiptoes out, as if she didn't want to disturb the ashes on the carpet. Turning back to* BURKE, *she blows air kisses.)* I do hate to rush off like this! I wish I had more time to spend with you! Oh, oh, oh! Let me tell you something, I really do *hate* to leave you so *abruptly*!

*(*RIVER *exits.* BURKE *smiles, and then notices the ash on the glass display case. She runs her fingers and feels the ash between her thumb and forefinger. She turns around, gets some rubbing alcohol and a cloth. She begins to clean the ashes off.)*

Final Curtain

Playwright's note:

In life, Mark Hopkinson was partnered to Charles Nedrow. Both men were among the first wave of Americans to become infected with HIV. Mark died first, and Charles subsequently succumbed to AIDS.

Joan Rivers survived her friend Mark Hopkinson by more than twenty-six years, during which she overcame the existential crisis that engulfed her life in 1988. She reconciled with her daughter, came to terms with her husband's suicide, and revived her career. She became a cultural force in entertainment and was a ubiquitous presence in American society. She died September 4, 2014.